My Path to Math

123456789

FRACTIONS

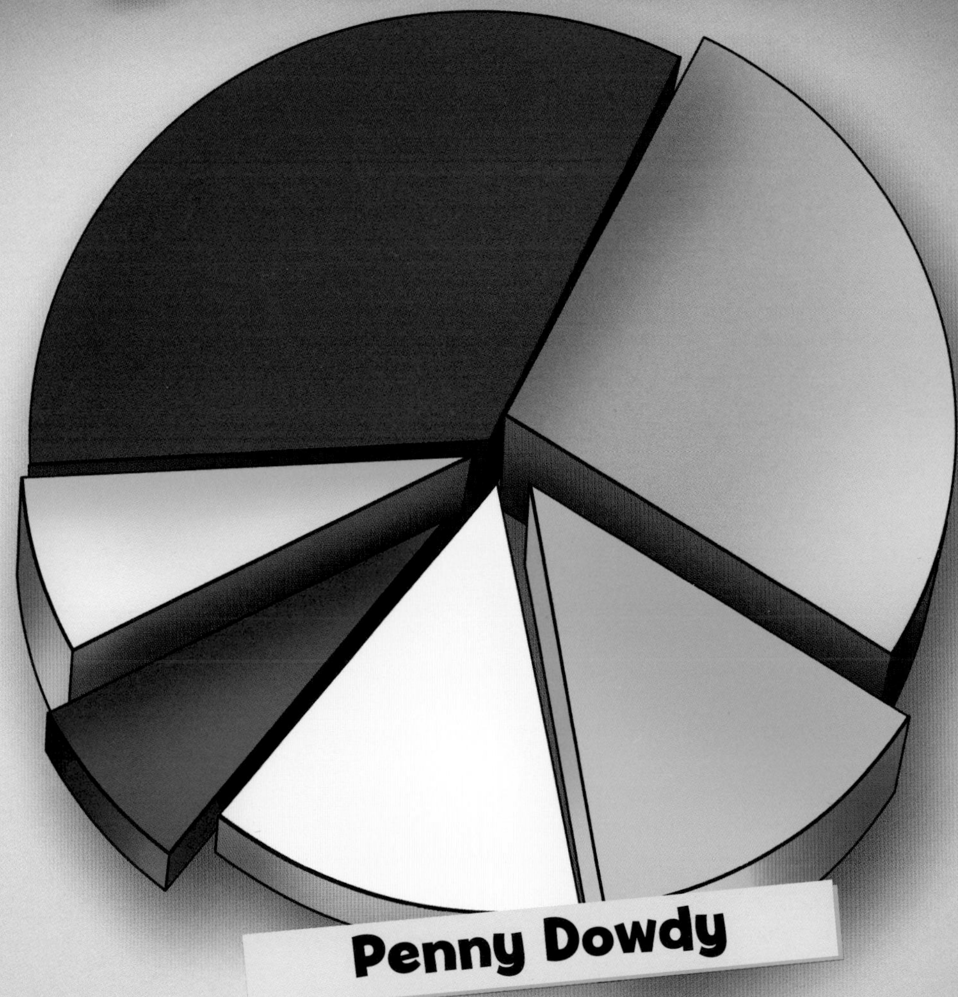

Penny Dowdy

Crabtree Publishing Company
www.crabtreebooks.com

Author: Penny Dowdy
Coordinating editor: Chester Fisher
Series editor: Jessica Cohn
Editors: Reagan Miller, Molly Aloian
Proofreader: Crystal Sikkens
Project coordinator: Robert Walker
Production coordinator: Margaret Amy Salter
Prepress technician: Margaret Amy Salter
Logo design: Samantha Crabtree
Cover design: Ranjan Singh (Q2AMEDIA)
Design: Tarang Saggar (Q2AMEDIA)
Project manager: Santosh Vasudevan (Q2AMEDIA)
Art direction: Rahul Dhiman (Q2AMEDIA)
Photo research: Anju Pathak (Q2AMEDIA)

Photographs:
© 123rf: Jingsen: p. 7
© Alamy: cover (apples)
© Istockphoto.com: Arpad Nagy Bagoly: p. 21, 23; Bluestocking: p. 19 (middle); Matjaz Boncina: p. 16, 17; João Paulo Calvet: p. 4 (right); Robert Gebbie: p. 4 (left); Christopher Ewing: p. 6; Terentyev Ilya: p. 15; Michal Kolosowski: p. 19 (top); Ljupco Smokovski: p. 19 (bottom); TSchon: p. 10
© Jupiter Images: BananaStock: cover (family); Jose Luis Pelaez, Inc: p. 5
© Q2AMedia: p. 1
© Shutterstock: Ilker Canikligil: p. 9; Katariina Järvinen: p. 20; Artsiom Kireyau: p. 13; Sylvain Legare: p. 14; Elena Moiseeva: p. 12; Jelena Popic: p. 11; South12th Photography: p. 8

Library and Archives Canada Cataloguing in Publication

Dowdy, Penny
Fractions / Penny Dowdy.

(My path to math)
Includes index.
ISBN 978-0-7787-4338-5 (bound).--ISBN 978-0-7787-4356-9 (pbk.)

1. Fractions--Juvenile literature. I. Title. II. Series: Dowdy, Penny. My path to math.

QA117.D69 2008 j513.2'6 C2008-906084-9

Library of Congress Cataloging-in-Publication Data

Dowdy, Penny.
Fractions / Penny Dowdy.
p. cm. -- (My path to math)
Includes index.
ISBN-13: 978-0-7787-4356-9 (pbk. : alk. paper)
ISBN-10: 0-7787-4356-X (pbk. : alk. paper)
ISBN-13: 978-0-7787-4338-5 (reinforced library binding : alk. paper)
ISBN-10: 0-7787-4338-1 (reinforced library binding : alk. paper)
1. Fractions--Juvenile literature. I. Title. II. Series.

QA117.D69 2008
513.2'6--dc22

2008040147

Crabtree Publishing Company

www.crabtreebooks.com 1-800-387-7650

Published in Canada
Crabtree Publishing
616 Welland Ave.
St. Catharines, Ontario
L2M 5V6

Published in the United States
Crabtree Publishing
PMB16A
350 Fifth Ave., Suite 3308
New York, NY 10118

Published in the United Kingdom
Crabtree Publishing
White Cross Mills
High Town, Lancaster
LA1 4XS

Published in Australia
Crabtree Publishing
386 Mt. Alexander Rd.
Ascot Vale (Melbourne)
VIC 3032

Contents

Lunchtime!

It is time for lunch. Mom says we will make fruit salad. She will help us cut the fruit.

She cuts the fruit into pieces that are the same size. This makes the salad easier to eat. Pieces that are the same size are called **equal parts**.

We use math
in the kitchen!

Equal Parts

Equal parts means the sizes are the same. You can make equal parts many different ways.

Two people who share an apple need two equal parts. They each get the same **amount**. Six friends who share an orange get six equal parts. Each part is a **fraction** of the whole.

What if two friends
shared the orange?

Halves

A **half** is one of two equal parts. If we put the two parts together, we have a whole.

Cut a watermelon in half and make two equal parts. Each part is called one-half. You can write one-half using numbers: 1/2.

whole

Activity Box

The bottom number in a fraction tells how many parts make a whole. The top number in a fraction tells how many parts you have.

Try writing the fraction for one-half.

Thirds

Three equal parts are **thirds**. Here is a bowl full of bits of **coconut**. **Split** it into three equal parts.

We write the fraction for each piece like this: 1/3. The bottom number tells how many parts make the whole: 3. The top part tells how many parts you have: 1.

Activity Box

Find a measuring cup.
Practice measuring one-third of a cup.

The circle shows
one-third of the big cup.

Two-Thirds

These are **pomegranate** seeds. We split one cup of seeds into three equal parts. Each part is one-third of a cup. We use two parts in the salad. That fraction looks like this: 2/3.

The top number of a fraction tells how many parts you have: 2. Not every fraction has the number 1 on top.

This circle shows two-thirds of the cup of seeds.

Fourths

Mom cuts a **kiwi** into four equal parts. She makes **fourths**. One-fourth will make one yummy bite.

We write the fraction one-fourth like this: 1/4. The top number tells how many parts we have: 1. The bottom number tells how many parts make a whole: 4.

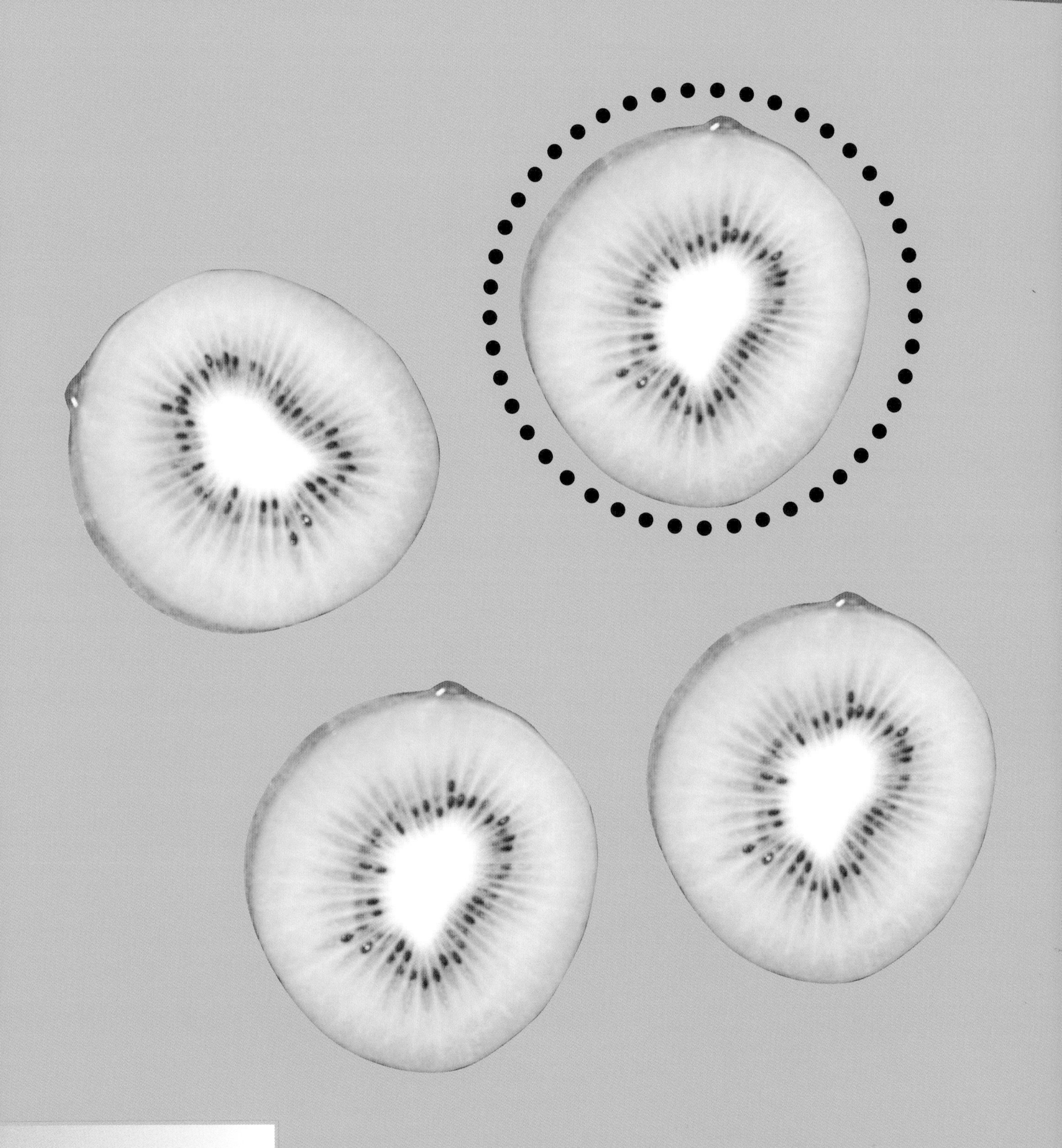

The circle shows
one-fourth of a kiwi.

More Fourths

We can break one thing into four parts. We call each part a fourth. One part of four things is called one-fourth or one-quarter. Two parts of four things is called two-fourths or one-half. Three parts of four things is called three-fourths or three-quarters.

The circle shows two-fourths
of the group of strawberries.
Two-fourths is one-half.

Different Sizes

Think about 1/2, 1/3, and 1/4 of an orange. These are three different sizes. Which is biggest?

Look at the bottom numbers. The more pieces you cut, the smaller the pieces are. A big number on the bottom means small pieces. So 1/2 is the biggest piece.

1/2
1/3
1/4
Which picture shows the smallest pieces?

The Salad Is Done!

Mom serves the salad at last! She fills three bowls with the same amount. What is that fraction?

Think about what you learned. She makes three equal parts. She makes thirds. If I get one bowl, I get 1/3. Yum!

Activity Box

Imagine if Mom used four bowls instead of three. What fraction would one bowl be?

Who gets the largest fraction of salad in this picture?

Glossary

amount A number of something

coconut A tree fruit with a hard shell and sweet white insides

equal parts Parts of an object or a group that are the same in size or number

fourth A fraction with four equal parts

fraction A number that shows parts of a whole or parts of a group

half A fraction with two equal parts

kiwi A brown, fuzzy fruit with sweet, green insides

pomegranate A round dark red fruit with sweet red insides

split To divide or cut into parts

third A fraction with three equal parts

Index

Printed in the U.S.A. — CG